BUKH DIESEL DV 8SME/ME
WERKSTATTHANDBUCH

BUKH DIESEL DV 8SME/ME WERKSTATTHANDBUCH

ISBN/EAN: 9783954271511
Erscheinungsjahr: 2012
Erscheinungsort: Bremen, Deutschland

© maritimepress in Europäischer Hochschulverlag GmbH & Co. KG, Fahrenheitstr. 1, 28359 Bremen. Alle Rechte beim Verlag und bei den jeweiligen Lizenzgebern.

www.maritimepress.de | office@maritimepress.de

Die Deutsche Bibliothek verzeichnet diesen Titel in der Deutschen Nationalbibliografie. Bibliografische Daten sind unter http://dnb.ddb.de verfügbar.

BUKH DIESEL DV 8SME/ME WERKSTATTHANDBUCH

Workshop Manual

DV 8 SME/ME

CONTENTS:

TECHNICAL DATA	Page 3
REPAIR AND OVERHAUL DATA	Pages 4 - 5 - 6
SPECIAL TOOLS	Page 7
DIFFERENCE BETWEEN DV8SME AND DV8ME	Page 9
CYLINDER HEAD	Section C
FUEL SYSTEM, COVERNOR AND CAMSHAFT	Section H
PISTON, CONNECTING ROD, CYLINDER AND CRANKSHAFT	Section IJ
CRANKCASE, END COVERS AND MAIN BEARINGS	Section L
LUBRICATING OIL SYSTEM	Section N
COOLING WATER SYSTEM	Section O
ELECTRICAL SYSTEM	Section P
GEAR BW 3	Section R
SAIL-DRIVE	Section S

DV 8 SME/ME
Technical data

ENGINE TYPE	DV8SME/ME
RPM UNLOADED	3150 RPM
RPM LOADED	3000 RPM
RPM IDLING	1000 RPM
NUMBER OF CYLINDERS	1
RATIO OF COMPRESSION	1 : 18.4
BORE	85 mm
STROKE	85 mm
STROKE VOLUME	482 cm^3
MAX. CONTINUOUS RATING	8.2 HP
MAX. TORQUE	2.53 kgm
PRINCIPLE OF OPERATING	4-stroke, diesel
COMBUSTION SYSTEM	Direct injection
COOLING SYSTEM	Direct seawater with thermostat
AIR CONSUMPTION FOR COMBUSTION	40 m^2/hour
MAX. INCLINATION, FORE	20°
MAX. INCLINATION, AFT	5°
MAX. INCLINATION, SIDEWAYS (port) (starboard)	25° 35°

A

DV 8 SME/ME

Repair and overhaul data

CYLINDER HEAD:

Inlet valve guide inside diameter	9.020 - 9.030 mm
Max. clearance valve/guide (inlet)	0.08 mm
Exhaust valve guide inside diameter	9.040 - 9.055 mm
Max. clearance valve/guide (exhaust)	0.10 mm
Distance between valve heads and the surface of the cylinder head	1.0 - 1.8 mm
Clearance between rocker arm and rocker shaft	0.045 - 0.070 mm
Valve adjustment (cold engine) inlet	0.20 mm
(cold engine) exhaust	0.25 mm
Torque moment (cylinder head)	7.0 kpm
Torque moment (fuel valve)	2.3 kgm

CYLINDER:

Diameter	85 mm
Clearance	0.06 mm
Max. wear and tear before exchange/repair	0.30 mm
Clearance between top of piston and top of cylinder	0.3 - 0.4 mm

PISTON:

Ring gap - compression rings (new)	0.35 - 0.55 mm
Ring gap - oil scraper ring (new)	0.25 - 0.40 mm
Ring gap - <u>exchange limit</u>	max. 2.0 mm

B   DV 8 SMÉ/ME

Repair and overhaul data

CONNECTING ROD:

Weight	800 g
Torque moment connecting rod screws	4.0 kgm

CRANKSHAFT:

Standard crank journal	42.000 mm
Standard connecting rod journal	45.000 mm
Undersize bearings for crank journal and connecting rod journal	0.25 - 0.50 - 0.75 mm
Clearance crank journal/bearing	0.030 - 0.086 mm
Clearance connecting rod journal/bearing	0.015 - 0.070 mm
End play for crankshaft	0.10 - 0.20 mm

FUEL SYSTEM:

Number of holes in nozzle	4
Protrusion of nozzle in cyl. head	3.5 - 4.0 mm
Opening pressure of fuel valve	210 - 220 kp/cm^2
Injection timing	$27° \pm 1°$ B.T.D.C. = flywheel measure 69 ± 2.5 mm = 5.9 mm before top measured on piston.

C DV 8 SME

Repair and overhaul data

TORQUE MOMENTS:

End cover towards coupling	2.3 kpm – 22.5 Nm
End cover towards flywheel	2.3 kpm – 22.5 Nm
Oil sump	0.8 kpm – 7.8 Nm
Nozzle holder in cylinder head	2.3 kpm – 22.5 Nm
Flexible coupling	6.0 kpm – 58.9 Nm
Connecting rod screw	4.0 kpm – 39.2 Nm
Cylinder head	7.0 kpm – 68.6 Nm
Flywheel	18.0 kpm – 176.6 Nm
S-drive leg for engine	4.2 kpm – 41.1 Nm

Special tools

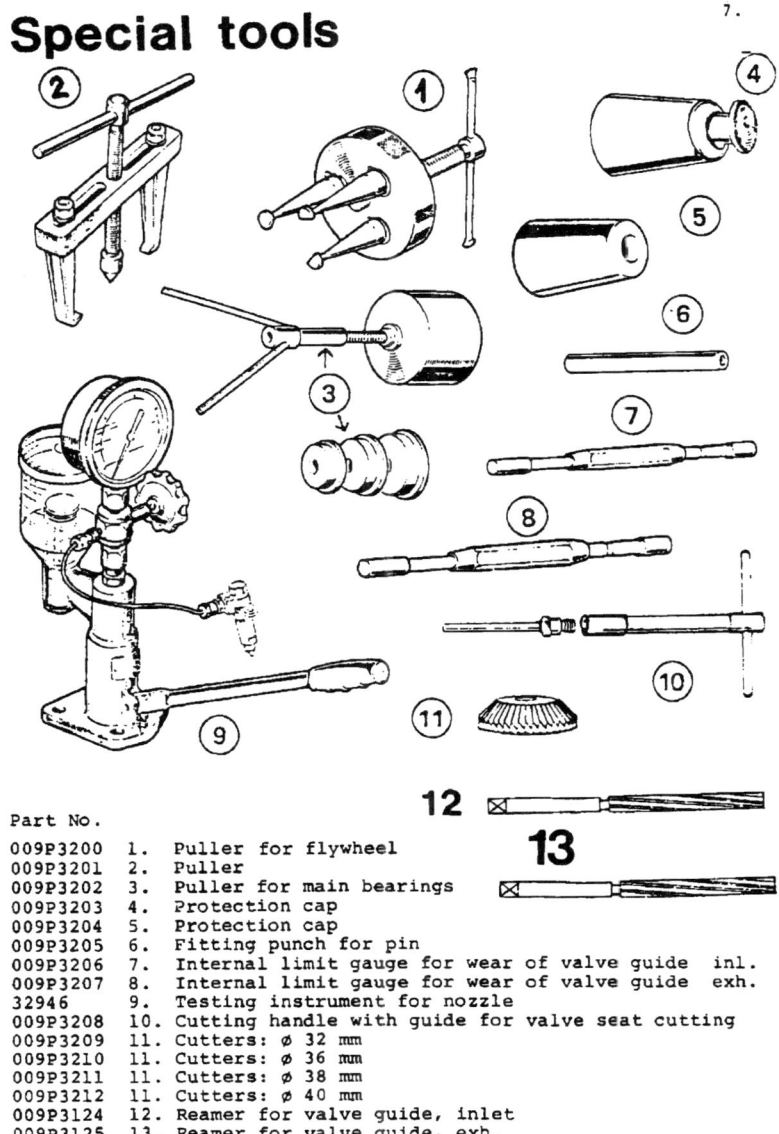

Part No.
```
009P3200   1.  Puller for flywheel
009P3201   2.  Puller
009P3202   3.  Puller for main bearings
009P3203   4.  Protection cap
009P3204   5.  Protection cap
009P3205   6.  Fitting punch for pin
009P3206   7.  Internal limit gauge for wear of valve guide  inl.
009P3207   8.  Internal limit gauge for wear of valve guide  exh.
32946      9.  Testing instrument for nozzle
009P3208  10.  Cutting handle with guide for valve seat cutting
009P3209  11.  Cutters: ø 32 mm
009P3210  11.  Cutters: ø 36 mm
009P3211  11.  Cutters: ø 38 mm
009P3212  11.  Cutters: ø 40 mm
009P3124  12.  Reamer for valve guide, inlet
009P3125  13.  Reamer for valve guide, exh.
```

8.

PREPARATION FOR DISMANTLING OF ENGINE

Remove the engine from the boat and drain off water and l oil and then the saildrive with intermediate housing and membrane should be dismantled from the engine unit.

Before the described dismantling is carried out pull off flywheel and alternator by means of a three-legged special puller.

Dismantle the coupling half for the flexible coupling from the opposite end of the engine and remove the engine brackets for fastening in the boat.

After that the engine should be fitted in a repair manipulator or at a file bench or something similar.

DIFFERENCES BETWEEN DV8SME AND DV8ME

This manual was originally prepared for DV8SME, however, it also applies to DV8ME, as among other things section R regarding the BW3 gearbox is included.

Besides the gearbox, DV8SME and DV8ME are different as to the construction, but alike as far as the repair is concerned.

Substantial differences in construction to be mentioned:

1. Number of balls for governor is different on the two engine types, as the DV8SME has 8 balls whereas DV8ME has 3 balls, thus the driver for the balls is different too.

2. The base cover for DV8ME has been changed compared to DV8SME, as the breather pipe on the "ME" has been moved to the vent cover, thus changing the construction as well, and the dip stick has been moved up on the side of the engine. Furthermore, an oil strainer is placed in the base cover of the "ME" type.

3. Further, the housing of the fuel pump is different, the connection being different. The other components are the same on both types.

SECTION C

CYLINDER HEAD

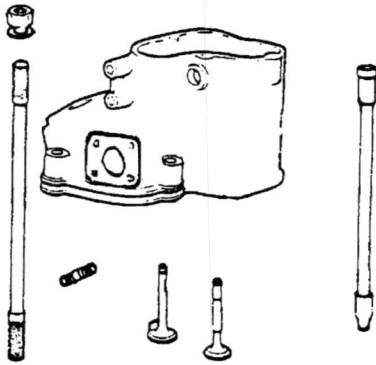

Contents:

Removal of cylinder head	page C 3
Dismantling of cylinder head	page C 3
Checking of valve guide	page C 3
Exchange of valve guide	page C 3
Checking of valves	page C 3
Cutting of valve seats	page C 4
Grinding of valves	page C 4
Checking of valve springs	page C 5
Checking of rocker shaft	page C 5
Bleeding valve	page C 5
Fitting of fuel valve	page C 5
Fitting of valves	page C 6
Checking of valve heads/ depth compared to upper surface	page C 6
Fitting of push rods	page C 6
Refitting of cylinder head	page C 6
Adjustment of valve clearance	page C 6

C3

Removal of Cylinder Head

1. Drain off water and oil from the engine.
2. Loosen the four nuts of the cylinder head and lift the cyl. head out.

Dismantling of Cylinder Head

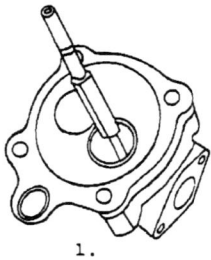

1.

1. Press out the rocker shaft and remove the rocker arms after the screw (3 mm Allen key) pos. A, sketch 2 has been loosened.
2. Dismantle the decompression valve by pulling the 3 mm lock-pin pos. B, sketch 2 up by means of a pair of tongs or something similar.
3. Remove the conical locking rings for the valves and then remove the valve springs, guides and valves.

   The head of the inlet valve is equipped with a fixed guard and a surface on the valve stem and thus the lower valve guide must be lifted and turned a half when dismantling the valve (valve guide pos. 3, sketch 2).

2.

Checking of Valve Guide (Sketch 1)

Examine the valve guides for wear and tear by means of an internal limit gauge, the "thick" end of which it must not be possible to fit in the valve guide hole.

See new measures and repair measures on page

Exchange of Valve Guide

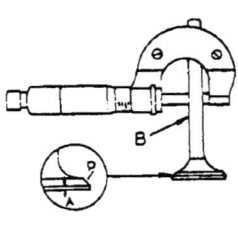

3.

Press out or knock out the valve guides by means of a punch and a hammer.

Press in new valve guides considering the pressing-in dimensions as before the dismantling.

For reaming of the guides use p/N 009P3124 for inlet and p/N 009P3125 for exhaust.

A cooling of the valves before the refitment in a deep freezer or with CO_2 would be an advantage.

Checking of Valves (Sketch 3)

4.

Check the condition of the valve by measuring A and B.

If the clearance between valve and guide is less than 0.08 mm (inlet) and 0.10 mm (exhaus and the wear of B less than 0.03 mm and A is bigger than 0.5 mm, the valves can be used.

C 4

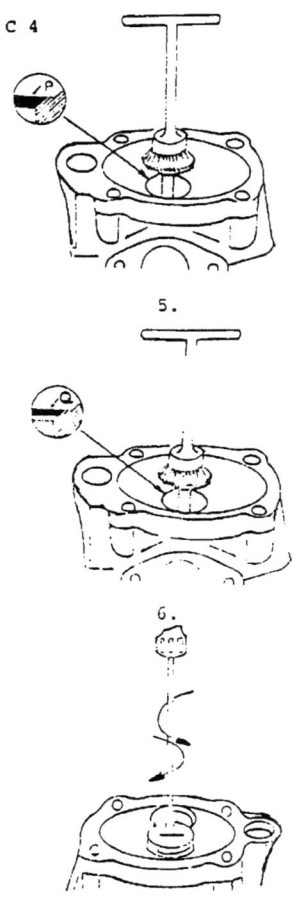

5.

6.

7.

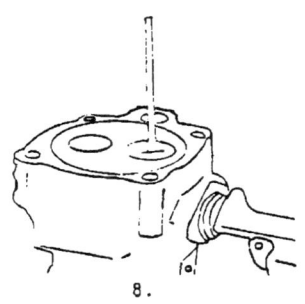

8.

Further see new measures and repair measures page 4.

Rake at P = 45°.

<u>Cutting of Valve Seats (Sketches 5 and 6)</u>

On engines which have been running for a longer period or which have "burns" on the contact face a refacing of the valve seats is necessary.

This is done by means of a valve cutter with fixed guide.

By cutting of the valve seats the valve seat surface P (sketch 5) widens and the opening of the valve becomes smaller.

If the surface P is more than 2.0 mm wide the seat is cut with the opposite cutter of the cutter in order to increase the Q-clearance and the valve seat surface is reduced to ideal measure 1.2 - 1.3 mm.

If the valves have often been ground and the seats cut, the valves will sink lower down in the seats, and thus the compression room will be increased.

This may result in the fact that it may be necessary to exchange the valve seats.

<u>The depth of the valve seats compared to the surface of the cylinder head is on a new engine 0.9 - 1.1 mm.</u>

<u>Grinding of Valves</u>

Grind the valves with abrasive compound as indicated on sketches 7 and 8.

C 5

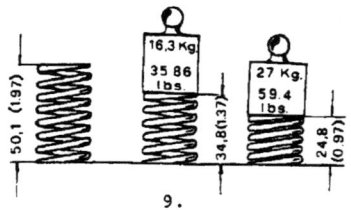

9.

Checking of Valve Springs

In order to check possible defects on the springs, these may be loaded by weights as indicated on sketch 9.

Clearance for load and length is +/- 10%.

Exchange the springs if the values indicated cannot be obtained.

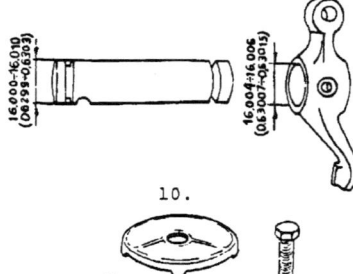

10.

Checking of Rocker Arm

Check the wear and tear between arm and shaft (sketch 10).

Max. wear between arm and shaft is 0.15 mm.

Axial clearance should be 0.20 - 0.40 mm.

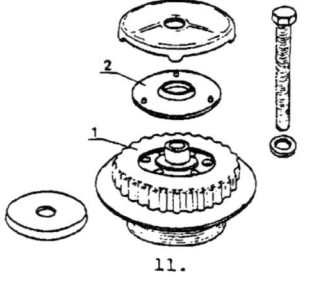

11.

Bleeding Valve (Sketch 11)

The bleeding valve is placed on the side of the engine and at the same time it serves as oil filling cap.

Clogging of the valve will cause an excess pressure in the engine resulting in lubricating oil leakage and thus the valve should occasionally be cleaned in cleaning fluid at repairs when it has been taken apart

Fitting of Fuel Valve

The protrusion of the fuel valve in the cyl. head measure S, sketch 12 is to be 3.5 - 4.0 mm.

The protrusion should be adjusted by means of copper rings which are placed between the contact face between the fuel valve and the cyl. head, as indicated on sketch 13.

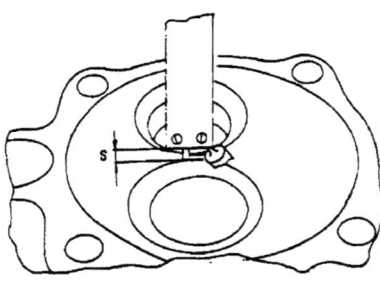

12.

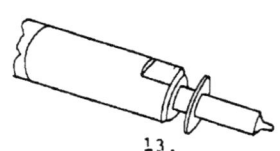

13.

C 6

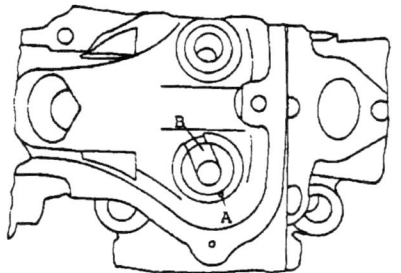

14.

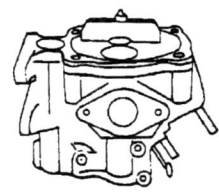

15.

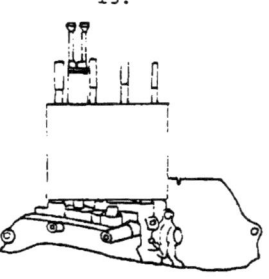

16.

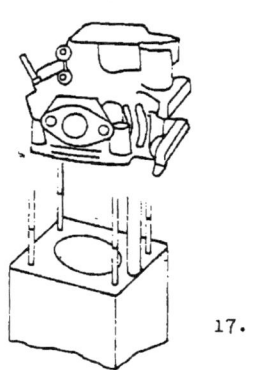

17.

Fitting of Valves

As mentioned under "Dismantling of Cylinder Head" page C 3, a guard is fitted on the head of the inlet valve.

On sketch 14 pos. A is indicating the lock pin for the valve spring guide and pos B. the recess in the valve spring guide fitting into the milled surface on the valve stem.

By fitting, the valve spring guide should be turned a half before it is placed around the valve stem and is put down around the lock pin in correct position.

Finally the springs of the valves, upper valve spring guide and the conical locking halves are fitted.

Checking of the Depth of the Valve Heads Compared to the Surface of the Cylinder Head

As mentioned under "Cutting of Valve Seats" page C 4 the depth on new engines is 0.9 - 1.1 mm.

The max. wear is a depth of 1.8 mm which can be measured by means of a measuring bridge as indicated on sketch 15.

Fitting of Push Rods

When fitting the push rods (sketch 16 it should be observed that the push rod which is nearest to the cylinder is for the inlet and the one farest away is for the exhaust. When being inattentive it may be possible to exchange the push rods by mistake.

Fitting of Cylinder Head

Put on the cyl. head gasket and fit the cyl. head and tighten it by 7 k]

Adjusting of Valve Clearance

Adjust the valve clearance at

(cold engine) inlet   0.20 mm
(cold engine) exhaust 0.25 mm

SECTION H

Fuel System
Governor
Camshaft

H 2

Contents:

Fuel valve	page H 3
Adjustment of injection pressure	page H 3
Cleaning of nozzle holes	page H 3
Testing of fuel valve	page H 3
Fuel lift pump	page H 4
Dismantling of fuel lift pump	page H 4
Fitting of fuel lift pump	page H 4
Fuel pump	page H 5
Checking of pump pressure	page H 5
Dismantling of fuel pump	page H 5
Calibration of pump	page H 5
Assembling of fuel pump	page H 6
Refitment of fuel pump	page H 7
Adjustment of injection timing	page H 8
Adjustment of fuel quantity	page H 8
Dismantling of governor	page H 10
Refitment of governor	page H 10
Dismantling of camshaft	page H 10
Refitment of camshaft	page H 10

H 3

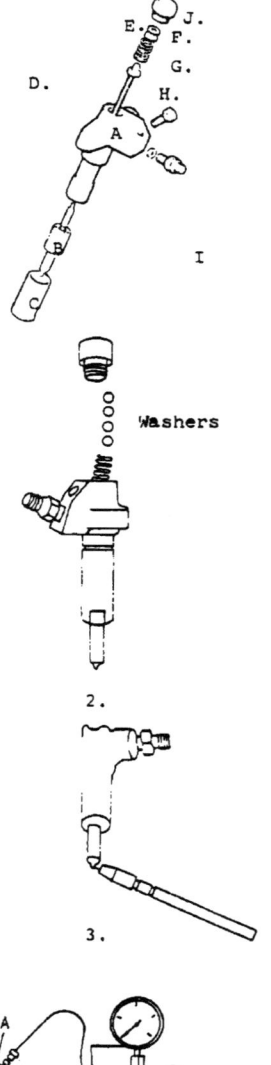

Fuel Valve

On sketch 1 the following is indicated:

A. Nozzle holder
B. Nozzle with needle
C. Union nut
D. Return oil connection
E. Spring washer
F. Washers for adjustment
G. Spring
H. Pressure pin
I. Connection
J. Pressure union (plug)

Adjustment of Injection Pressure

The injection pressure should be 210-220 kp/cm^2 and should be adjusted by means of shims as indicated on sketch 2.

Cleaning of Nozzle Holes

The nozzle holes can be cleaned with cleaning wire with a diameter of 0.28 mm.

Testing of Fuel Valve

Test the fuel valve in a nozzle testing apparatus for tightness, opening at correct pressure as indicated above and as to uniform spray angle of the fuel.

17

H 4

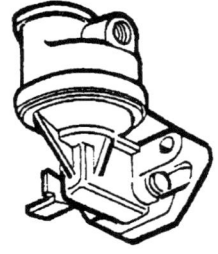

5.

Fuel Lift Pump

The fuel lift pump is driven on the same sidemounted arrangement as the cooling water pump.

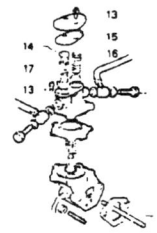

6.

Dismantling of Fuel Lift Pump

Dismantle the pump according to sketch 6.

This only applies to the first 25 engines. After these engines the pump is burred-up and cannot be dismantled.

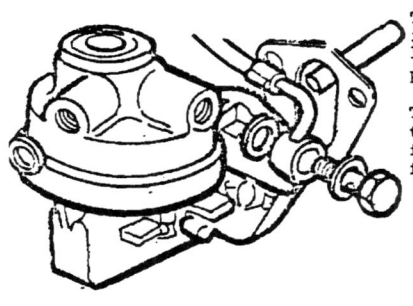

7.

Fitting of Fuel Lift Pump

The diaphragm of the pump shall have an initial tension of 0.5-0.7 mm with at least one gasket fitted and with the push rod in the lowest position.

This may be checked by measuring before the pump is fitted or by means of a feeler gauge while the pump is loosened from its attachment.

H 5

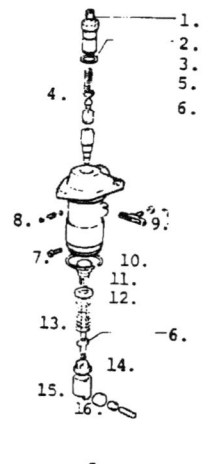

Fuel Pump

On sketch 9 the following is indicated:

1. Union nut for fuel pressure pipe
2. Seal ring
3. Pressure spring
4. Gasket
5. Delivery valve with seat
6. Pump element compl.
7. Lock screw
8. Eccentric adjusting screw
9. Regulating quadrant
10. Locking ring
11. Adjusting bushing
12. Spring plate
13. Piston spring
14. Spring plate
15. Roller cage
16. Roller/bushing/shaft

Checking of Pump Pressure

Fit a manometer with measuring range up to 600 kg/cm^2 while the pump is placed on the engine.

Turn the flywheel slowly so that the pump is activated with one stroke of pump. In doing so the throttle control should be activated.

If the pressure is lower than 300 kg/cm^2 the complete pump element should be replaced.

During the checking the indicator on the manometer will show a temporary increase of the pressure to a max. value and after that, the pressure will suddenly drop and remain at a lower pressure.

If the pressure drop is bigger than 50 kg/cm^2 only the delivery valve with seat should be replaced.

Dismantling of Fuel Pump

Dismantle the pump acc. to the sketches. The lock screw pos. 7, sketch 8 and the locking ring pos. 10 should be removed together with the union nut pos. 1.

Calibration of Pump

The delivered quantity of fuel of the pump is adjusted by means of the eccentric screw pos. Q, sketch 9, so that the pump at 1000 working strokes with the toothed quadrant in max. position and without using the excess fuel device is giving 45-50 cm^3.

H 6

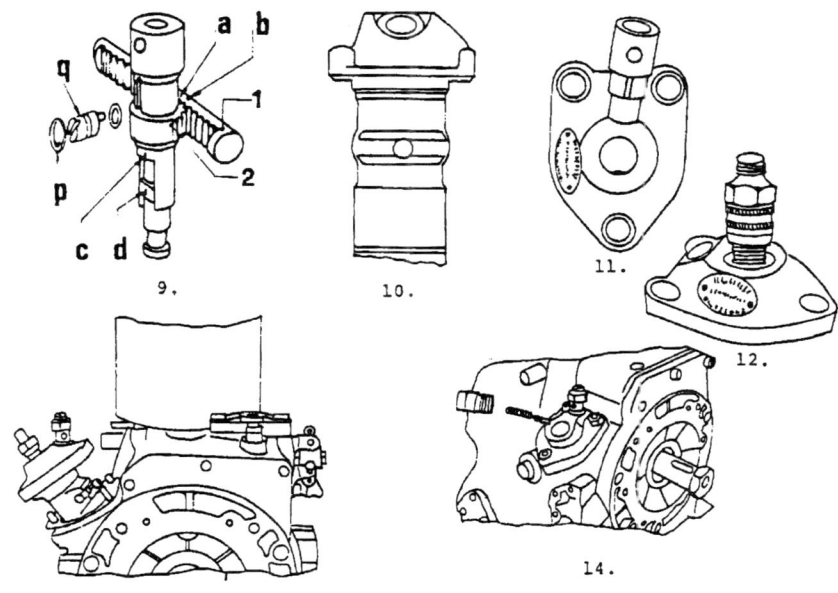

9. 10. 11. 12. 14. 15.

Assembling of Fuel Pump

1. Fit the element in the pump housing as shown on sketch 11 with the fuel inlet hole at right angles to the inlet connection of the pump housing.

    This position is necessary on account of the eccentric screw in the pump housing.

2. Fit the pressure valve with seat and union nut for pressure pipe provisionally to avoid that the element falls out (sketch 12).

3. Fit the toothed quadrant and lock it in the centre position as shown on sketch 10.

    Check that the toothed quadrant is operating easily in the guide.

4. The mark B on the toothed quadrant is to correspond with the mark A on the tooth arc as shown on sketch 9 and marks C and D are to correspond as well.

5. Fit the pump piston with the key placed in the same direction as the eccentric screw in the pump housing.

6. Assemble the piston spring of the pump, the roller guide arrangement and the spring plate acc. to sketch 8 and see to it that the parts are not changed about thus changing the injection measures.

7. In case of exchange of old pump for a new one it should be checked that:

    the distance between the injection cam in the bottom dead centre and the contact flange on the pump is between 82.6-83.0 mm as stated on the name plate of the pump.

  b. the piston stroke from the bottom dead centre on the cam to the beginning of the delivery is 2.20-2.30 mm.

8. When repairing and refitting an old pump check the pressure tightness as described on page H 5 "Checking of Pump Pressure".

Refitment of Fuel Pump

1. Fit the pump in the crankcase, fitting 2-3 shims (see page H 8 regarding adjusting of the injection timing), shown on sketch 16.

   In order to make the fitting of the pump easier turn the flywheel so that the cam for activating of the pump gets in a position of rest, i.e. in the bottom position.

   Place the toothed quadrant as shown on sketches 10 and 15 in the centre position during the fitting procedure.

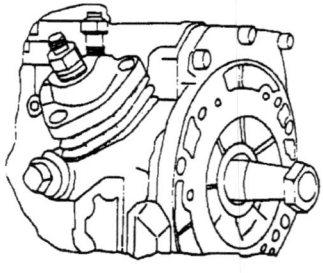

16.

Adjusting of Injection Timing (Sketches 17 and 18)

1. Remove pressure valve and pressure valve spring temporarily as stated on sketch 14. The pressure valve seat remains in the pump.

2. Put the throttle control in max. position.

3. Set the engine piston at compression stroke.

4. Fit injection timing indicator or a drip pipe on the pressure outlet of the fuel pump.

5. Either remove the complete cylinder head or a valve spring and let the valve "step" on the piston. Fit correspondingly a dial indicator so <u>the exact TOP position in the compression stroke is found</u> (do not forget to compensate for the play of the engine by turning over the flywheel and turning it back).

   Mark the flywheel for the top position opposite a fitted arrow (steel wire or something similar).

6. Turn the flywheel anti-clockwise until the "injection timing indicator" or the drip pipe registers the spill-time of the pump.

   (The needle drops on the "injection timing indicator"/ the fuel begins to run/drip out of the drip pipe).

7. The injection timing should be $27\pm1°$ before TOP in the compression stroke.

   $27\pm1°$ = <u>Flywheel measure 69 ± 2.5 mm before TOP (arc measure)</u>.

   $27\pm1°$ = <u>The distance of the piston before TOP 5.9 mm$\pm$4 mm</u>.

8. Adjust the pump with shims as shown on sketch 16. (Pls. see page H 7 regarding "Refitment of Fuel Pump" too).

Adjustment of Fuel Quantity

This is set at BUKH by testing with measured load at a test bench. If a test bench is not available, the following instructions may be used:

1. Turn the flywheel CLOCKWISE from the point when the injection begins (sketch 18) until the needle on the injection timing indicator falls, i.e. the injection has stopped.
   This point is to lie 13° <u>after the beginning of the injection</u>.
   13° = <u>flywheel measure 33 mm after beginning of injection</u>.

The duration of the injection and thus the effect is set at the eccentric screw at the governor as shown on sketch 20, 21, 22 and 23.

On the first approx. 50 DV8 engines the eccentric screw was hydraulically activated from the lub. oil system as shown on sketch 22 and after these approx. 50 engines it is mechanical.

In both cases the adjustment should be carried out by loosening the counter nut and turning the screw as shown on sketch 21.

In case of hydraulic activation remove the hose and activate the pin of the screw manually.

H

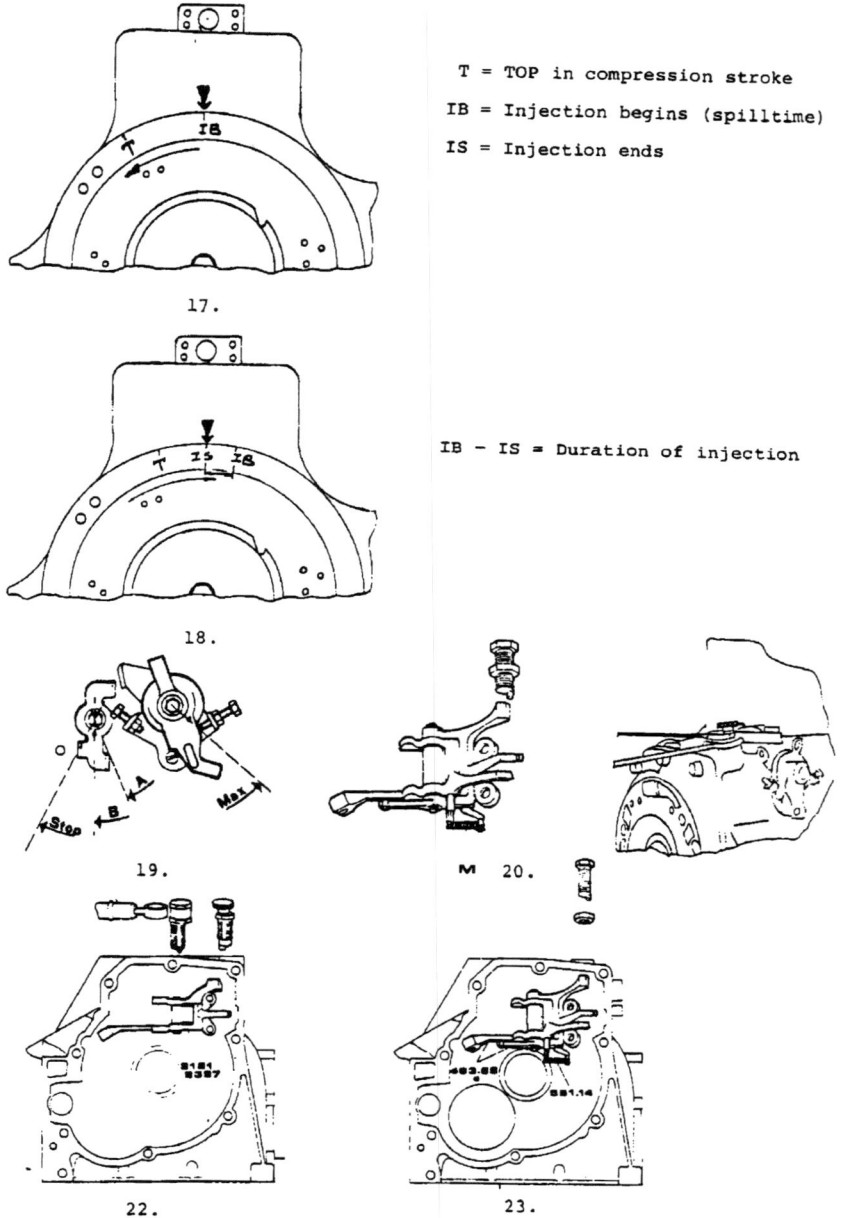

T = TOP in compression stroke
IB = Injection begins (spilltime)
IS = Injection ends

IB - IS = Duration of injection

H 10

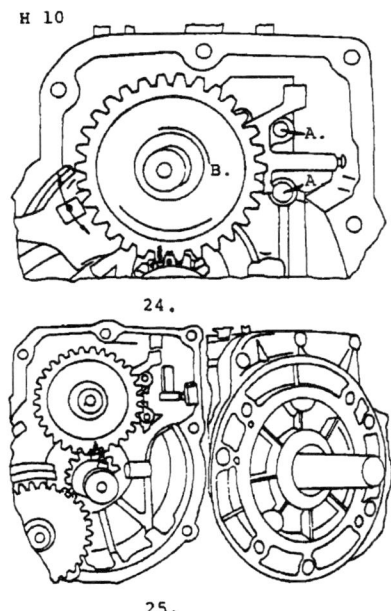

24.

25.

Dismantling of Governor

1. Unscrew the Allen screws pos. A, sketch 24 and lift out the governor pos. B together with the governor arm.

Refitment of Governor

The refitment is carried out in revers order, the fastening of the governor arm being carried out with an even distribution of the clearances at the screws A.

Check that the governor is moving freely and easily and that the spring is correctly placed at the end of the arm (see below).

Dismantling of Camshaft

Lift the camshaft free after the end cover has been removed.

Refitment of Camshaft

When refitting the camshaft and the governor shaft the centre marks must correspond with each other as stated on sketch 25.

When fitting the end cover over the gear wheels fit a protection cap on the crankshaft as stated on the right-hand picture at sketch 25 (also see section L page 5).

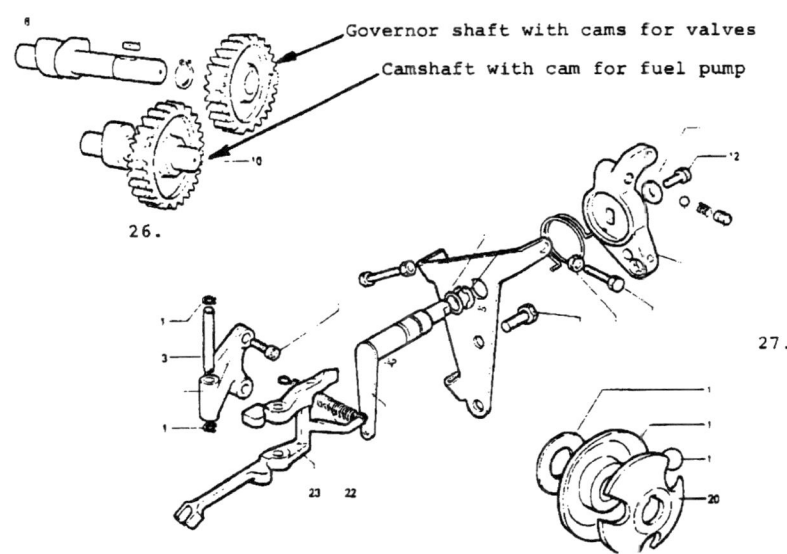

Governor shaft with cams for valves

Camshaft with cam for fuel pump

26.

27.

SECTION IJ

Piston, Connecting Rod, Cylinder and Crankshaft

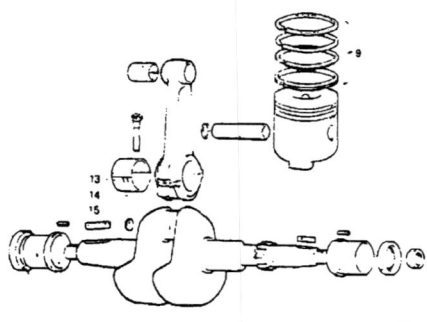

IJ 2

Contents:

Dismantling of cylinder	page IJ 3
Checking of cylinder	page IJ 3
Boring of cylinder	page IJ 3
Fitting of cylinder liner	page IJ 3
Dismantling of connecting rod	page IJ 4
Connecting rod bearings	page IJ 4
Refitment of connecting rod	page IJ 4
Dismantling of piston	page IJ 5
Fitting of piston	page IJ 5
Fitting of piston rings	page IJ 5
Placing of piston rings	page IJ 5
Dismantling of crankshaft	page IJ 6
Crankshaft	page IJ 6
Grinding of crankshaft	page IJ 6
Oil groove of crankshaft	page IJ 6
Fitting of crankshaft	page IJ 7
Grinding dimensions for crankshaft	page IJ 7
Oversize bearings	page IJ 7

IJ 3

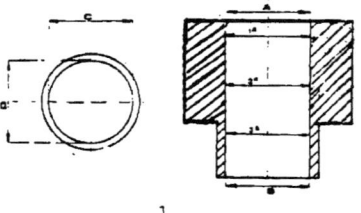

1.

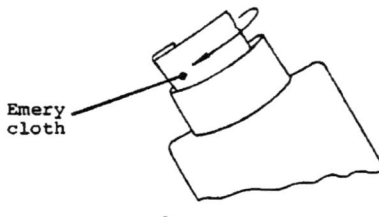

Emery cloth

2.

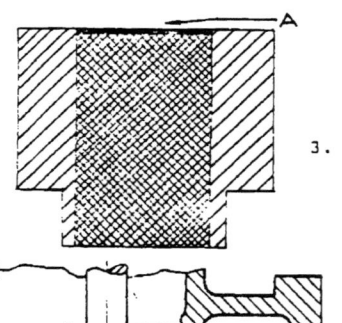

3.

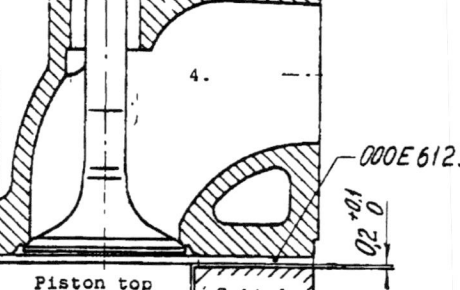

4.

Piston top   Cylinder

000E 6123

$0.2^{+0.1}_{0}$

Dismantling of Cylinder

1. Remove the cylinder head (sectio
2. Lift the cylinder liner free of the engine block. This may be done with or without the piston and the connecting rod placed.

Checking of Cylinder

Measure two diameters (C-D, sketch in three different heights with a dial gauge.

Max. conicity (A-B) and ovalness (C-D) is 0.06 mm.

If the cylinder is in order acc. to the above, it can be refitted perpa with new piston rings, and thus tri the cylinder with a piece of emery cloth (fineness 80-100) moistened w oil (sketch 2).

The trimming of the cylinder must result in a surface in the cylinder stated on sketch 3.

Boring of Cylinder

If the cylinder is damaged in the area A, sketch 3, the cylinder may l honed, proper consideration being hac to the piston ring gaps.

When starting printing this worksho; manual (June, 1982) no decision has been made regarding the introductio of oversize piston rings and theref(please contact BUKH on this subject before doing any repairs in case of problems with the cylinder.

Fitting of Cylinder Liner

1. At shims as shown on sketch 5 adjust so that there is 0.2-0.3 mm between piston head and cylinder as shown on sketch 4.

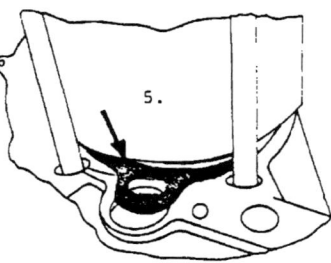

5.

IJ 4

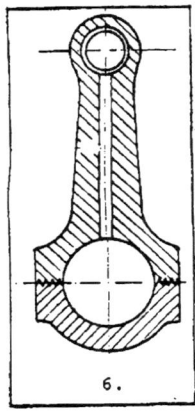

6.

Dismantling of Connecting Rod

1. Remove the base cover of the engine (the one pointing forward in the boat).
2. Loosen the screws for the connecting rod and remove connecting rod with cap and bearing.
3. Press the connecting rod with piston out above the cylinder if this has not been removed previously.

Connecting Rod Bearings

The connecting rod bearings are available in 0.25, 0.50 and 0.75 mm undersize.

Connecting rod journal is standard 45.000 mm.

See also regarding bearings page IJ 7.

Refitment of Connecting Rod

When refitting the connecting rod the numbers shall turn to the same side as stated on sketch 8.

Tigthen the screws for the connecting rod with a torque of 4.0 kpm.

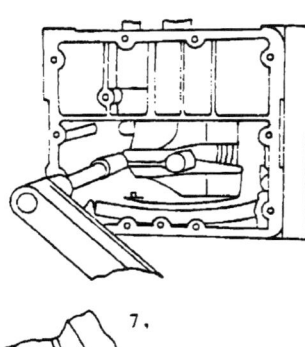

7.

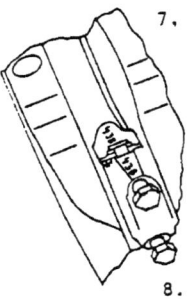

8.

IJ 5

Dismantling of Piston

Remove the connecting rod and the piston.

1. Remove one of the locking rings in the piston.
2. Press out the gudgeon pin A sketch 9.

Fitting of Piston

Fitting of piston is carried out in the reverse order of the above-mentioned, the piston being heated before the fitting on a boiling plate or something similar.

Fitting of Piston Rings

Fit the rings to the piston as stated on sketch 11:

1. Compression ring (chrome)
2. Compression ring
3. Compression ring with step turning downwards.
4. Oil scraper ring with chamfered edge turning upwards.

Exchange the piston rings if the piston ring gap exceeds 2 mm.

Check of wear of piston rings in the keyways in the piston: Sketch 10.

The rings shall be able to move free in the keyways of the piston.

Measure the clearance with a feeler gauge.

1. Compression ring, A-measure max. 0.22 mm
2. Compression ring, B-measure max. 0.18 mm
3. Compression ring, C-measure max. 0.18 mm
4. Scraper ring,   D-measure max. 0.16 mm

Placing of Piston Rings

When fitting the piston or the cylinder if this is fitted at last, the piston rings should be placed as shown on sketch 12.

The first and third piston ring should be turned $15°$ each opposite each other compared to the gudgeon pin.

The second and fourth piston ring shall be turned $180°$ compared to the first and third ring.

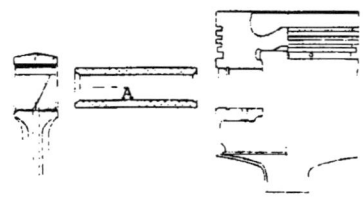

9.

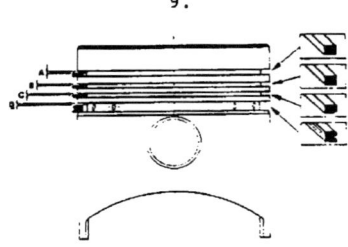

10.

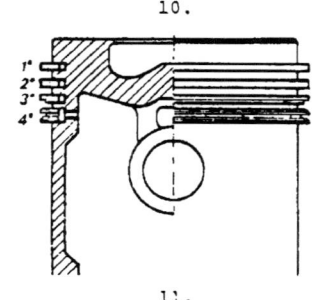

11.

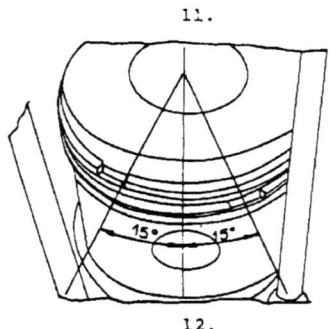

12.

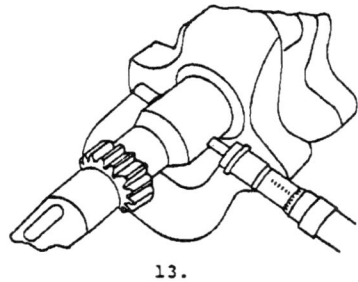

13.

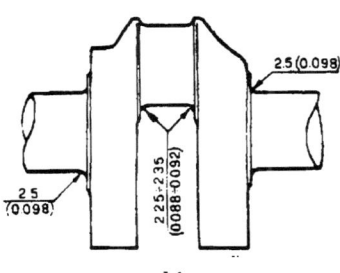

14.

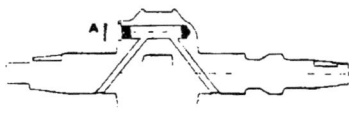

15.

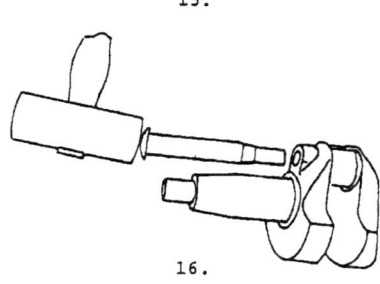

16.

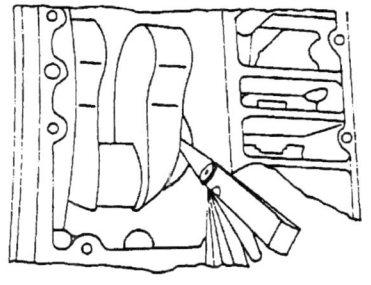

17.

Dismantling of Crankshaft

1. Remove cylinder head, connecting rod with piston and cylinder.
2. Remove flywheel and end covers and take out the crankshaft.

Crankshaft

The crankshaft is drop-forged and contrary to all other BUKH crankshafts it is tempered in 2.5 mm depth, i.e. that a re-tempering by grinding to even the largest undersize is not necessary.

Check of Crankshaft (Sketch 13)

Measure the crankshaft with a micrometer screw gauge and in case of max. 0.10 wear and tear the crankcase should be ground acc. to grinding data on page IJ 7.

Grinding of Crankshaft

When grinding the crankshaft acc. to the grinding data stated on page IJ 7, NO RADIUS MATERIAL must be removed from the journals or the axial clearance will change.

The roundness of the grindstone must not be under 3.0 mm (sketch 14 -2.5 mm), as otherwise there will be a risk of notch effects of the crankshaft.

Oil Groove of Crankshaft

On sketch 15 the groove of the crankshaft with plug A is shown. At greater repairs remove the expansion disc and clean the grooves.

At fitting of a new disc, as shown on sketch 16 (hammer, punch and expansion disc) the contact face should be cleane carefully before the fitting and smear the expansion disc with Lock-Tite or another lock liquid before fitting.

Fitting of Crankshaft

1. Fit the crankshaft in the crankcase with fitted protection caps at the ends in order to avoid damage of the main bearings and seal rings.
2. Fit the end cover (at flywheel end) with gasket.
3. Check the axial play of the crankshaft with a feeler gauge as shown on sketch 17. Adjust the axial play with the thickness of the gasket between the crankcase and the end cover.

THE AXIAL PLAY is to be 0.10-0.20 mm when the end cover is tightened with a torque of 2.3 kpm.

Grinding Dimensions for Crankshaft

STANDARD	UNDERSIZE			JOURNAL
	0.25	0.50	0.75	
44.994-45.010	44.744-44.760	44.494-44.510	44.244-44.260	Con. rod journal
41.984-42.000	41.734-41.750	41.484-41.500	41.234-41.250	Main bearing jour
CLEARANCE between bearing and crankshaft: 0.030-0.086 mm				Main bearing
CLEARANCE between bearing and crankshaft: 0.015-0.070 mm				Con. Rod journal

Oversize Bearings (Main bearing bushes)

The crankshaft is made from aluminium and in consequence of this the fitting hole in both the crankcase and end cover may be too "big" at repeated exchanges of bearings. Therefore it is possible to buy oversize bearings as to the outer diameter of the bearing, as stated below.

Outer diameter standard: 50.010 - 50.030 mm
1 mm oversize: 51.010 - 51.030 mm.

Exchange of bearings: See section L - Crankcase and end covers.

SECTION L

Crankcase, End Covers and Main Bearings

Contents:

Crankcase	page L 3
Dismantling of Bearing in Crankcase	page L 3
Dismantling of Bearing in End Cover	page L 3
Fitting of Main Bearing in End Cover	page L 4
Fitting of Main Bearing in Crankcase	page L 4
Dismantling of Lubricating Oil Pressure Relief Valve	page L 4
Fitting of Lubricating Oil Pressure Relief Valve	page L 5
Fitting of End Covers	page L 5

L 3

Crankcase

The crankcase and the two end covers shown and the bottom cover are made from aluminium.

The cover pos. 2 is towards the flywheel side and the cover pos. 5 is towards the S-drive.

The gasket pos. 3 is used as mentioned in section IJ page 7 for adjustment of the axial play of the crankshaft.

1.

Dismantling of Main Bearing in Crankcase

1. Remove flywheel, end covers and crankshaft.
2. Pull out the bearing in the crankcase by means of a special puller.

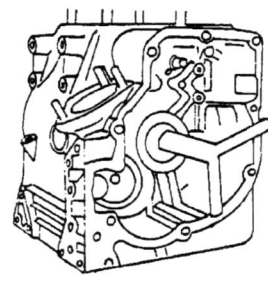

2.

Dismantling of Main Bearing in End Cover

1. Remove end cover (towards the flywheel)
2. Fit end cover in a vise and pull out the bearing with a special puller.

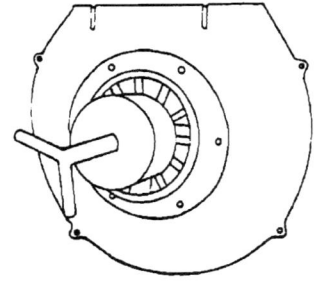

3.

OVER- AND UNDERSIZE BEARINGS: See S E C T I O N IJ under the crankshaft.

L 4

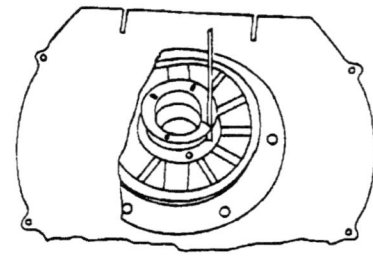

4.

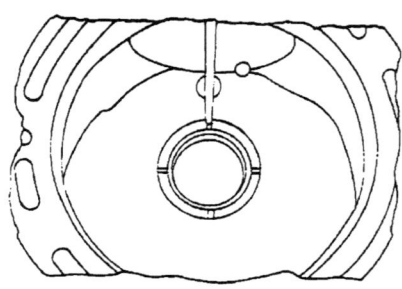

5.

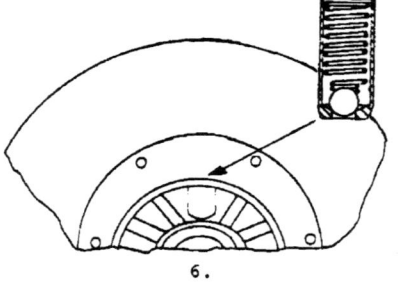

6.

Fitting of Main Bearing in
End Cover

1. Heat the end cover in a heater
   or in boiling water (to approx.
   $80°C$).

2. Cool the main bearing in a
   freezer or with CO_2.

3. Fit the bearing in the end
   cover, lining up the slots for
   the flex. lock-pins with the
   pins which have been fitted
   earlier.

Fitting of Main Bearing in
Crankcase

1. Heat crankcase to approx. $80°$
   as stated above.

2. Cool the main bearing as st?*
   above.

3. Fit the bearing in the crankcase in a similar way as stated
   above for the end cover.

Dismantling of Lubricating Oil
Pressure Relief Valve

The lub. oil pressure relief valve,
which is also dealt with in
section N, lub. oil system, is
fitted in the end cover at the
flywheel side.

1. Remove locking ring, spring
   and ball.

Fitting of Lubricating Oil Pressure Relief Valve

1. Check that the seat for the ball is clean and free from impurities.

2. Fit the ball, the spring and the locking ring.

Fitting of End Covers

When fitting the end covers it would be an advantage to use non-hardening sealing compound, e.g. CURIL K2 in connection with the gaskets pos. 3, sketch 1.

SECTION N

Lubricating Oil System

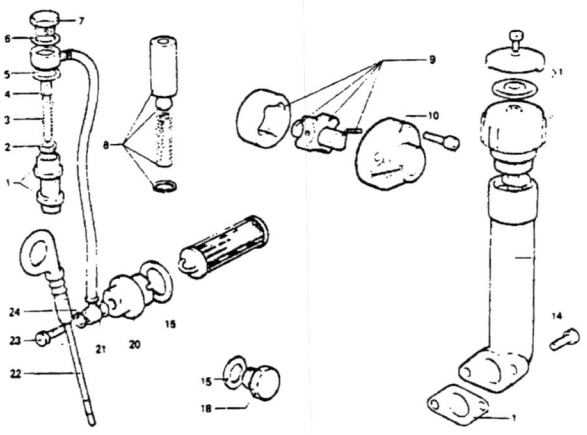

Contents

Lubricating oil system	page N 3
Qality of lubricating oil	page N 3
Change of lubricating oil	page N 3
Lubricating oil filter	page N 3
Dismantling of lubricating oil pump	page N 4
Refitment of lubricating oil pump	page N 4
Check of lubricating oil pump	page N 4
Dismantling of pressure relief valve	page N 5
Refitment of pressure relief valve	page N 5
Bottom cover	page N 5
Check of bottom cover	page N 5

N

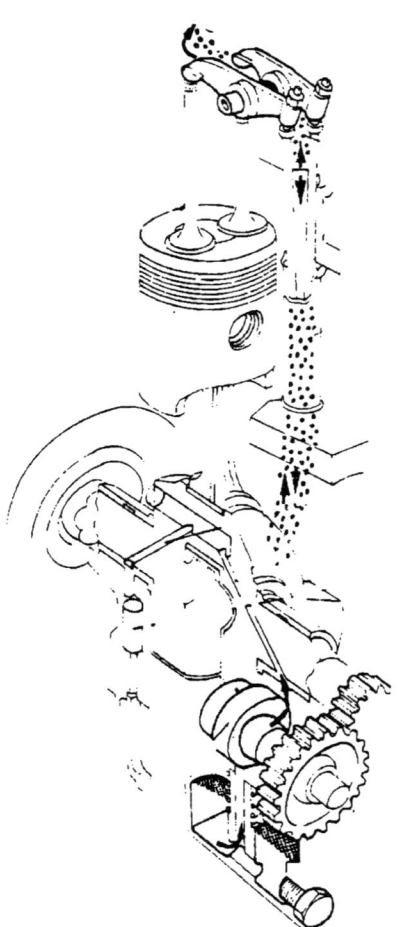

Lubricating Oil System

On the principle sketch the lubricating oil system is shown.

Main bearings, conn. rod bearing and gudgeon pin are pressure lubricated whereas the other component in the crankcase are lubricated by spray lubrication.

Lubricate the rocker arms with oil mist/oil vapour which goes up in a steam of hot air through the push rod room and runs back to the crankcase the same way.

Quality of Lubricating Oil

The quality of lubricating oil use is <u>API SERVICE CD OR CC</u> with a viscosity depending on the ambient air temperature. Oils (possible all-year oil) covering several viscosities may also be used.

Change of Lubricating Oil

The lub. oil is changed every 150 operating hours or once a year.

Fill 2.0 ltr. lub. oil on the engi equal to the upper mark on the dipstick.

Lubricating Oil Filter

A mesh filter is fitted in the engine block and this should only be cleaned in case of repairs of t engine when the filter is accessib

Dismantling of Lubricating Oil Pump

The lub. oil pump is placed in the crankcase and is accessible at:

1. Removal of S-drive and end cover.
2. Remove camshaft for the fuel pump.
3. Remove the cover of the lub. oil pump and remove the rotor ring.

Refitment of Lubricating Oil Pump

1. Fit the rotor ring in the crankcase with the chamfer towards the crankcase.
2. Fit the rotor and fix the cover so that the oil grooves correspond to those in the crankcase.

Check of Lubricating Oil Pump

1. Check the end play of the pump by means of a dial meter as shown on sketch 2.

   End play in new pump: <u>0.02-0.08 mm</u>

   Max. end play before exchange: <u>0.13 m</u>

Side play between rotor ring and pump housing (in the crankcase) is with new engine 0.139-0.189 mm.

<u>Max. side play before exchange:</u>
<u>0.339 mm.</u>

2. The pump having been taken apart: Check that the rotating parts of the pump are not worn or cracked.

In order to check the wear of the pump measure the dimensions on sketch 3 and in case of excess of the max. values mentioned below the parts should be exchanged.

C	max. 29.700 mm
D	max. 40.450 mm
E	max. 30.100 mm
F	max. 11.870 mm

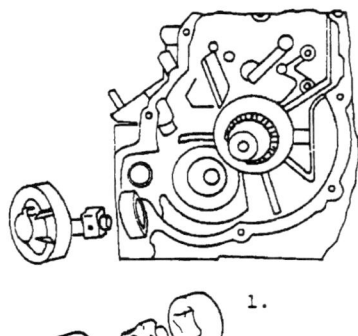

1.

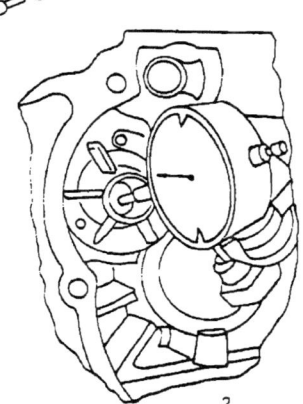

2.

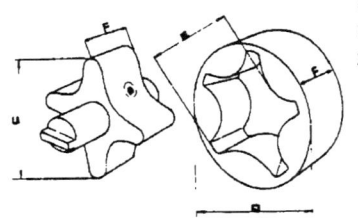

3.

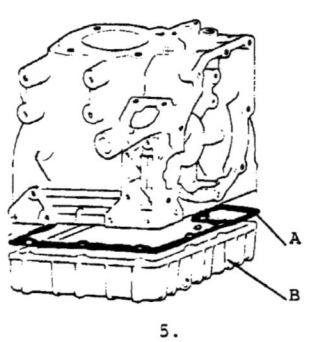

4.

5.

Dismantling of Pressure Relief Valve

1. Remove end cover at flywheel side.

2. Remove the locking ring, the spring and the ball on sketch 4.

Refitment of Pressure Relief Valve

1. Check that the seat for the ball is clean and free from impurities.

2. Fit the ball, the spring and the locking ring.

Bottom Cover

In the bottom cover, which will usuall be placed vertically ahead in the boat the suction pipe of the lub. oil pump is placed.

Therefore it is important when fitting the bottom cover to make sure that the gasket A, sketch 5, is correctly placed and packs round the aspirating hole.

Check of Bottom Cover

When dismantling the bottom cover chec the cover with a straight-edge in orde to check the height/the sealing possibility of the suction connection in proportion to the edge of the cover.

SECTION O

Cooling Water System

Contents

Cooling water system   page 0 3
Thermostat   page 0 3
Cooling water pump   page 0 3
Drawing of cooling water pump   page 0 4

O 3

Cooling Water System

The engine is with direct seawater cooling and thermostat. It is not possible to equip the engine with freshwater cooling, either with keel cooling or with heat exchanger.

Thermostat

The thermostat housing is placed in the cylinder head. The thermostat is a thermostat of the wax type with an opening temperature of approx. 60°C.

Sectional view
of thermostat
housing

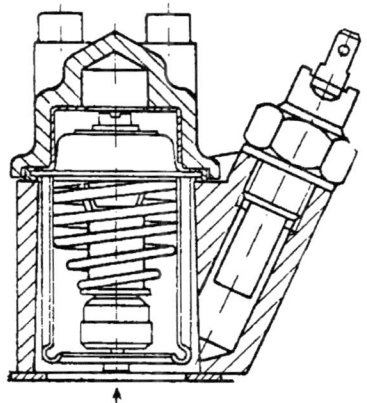

Transmitter
for cooling
water
temperature

Cooling Water Pump

The cooling water pump is an impeller pump with a capacity of 11 litres/min., It is the same pump which is used for DV10 and DV20 with direct seawater cooling.

The pump is driven as shown on the sketch below. A sketch of the pump is shown on page O 4.

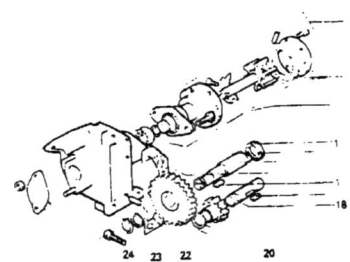

O 4

Cooling Water Pump for Direct Cooling

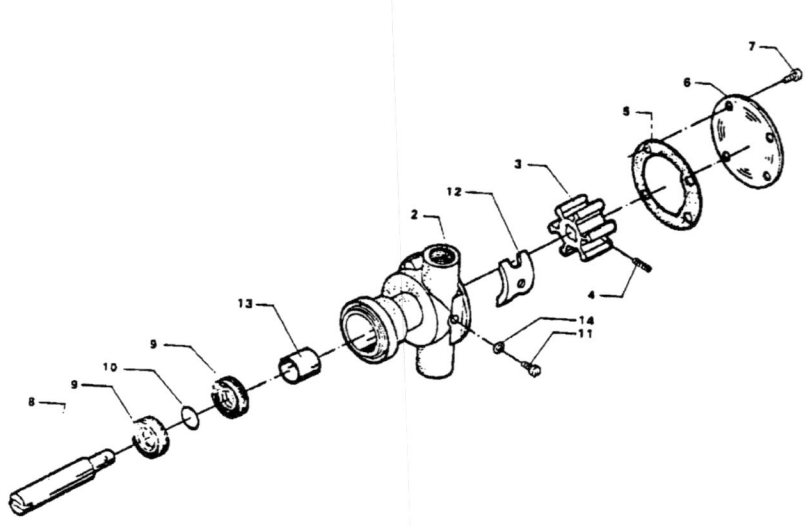

SECTION P

Electrical System

Contents

Wiring diagram   page P 3

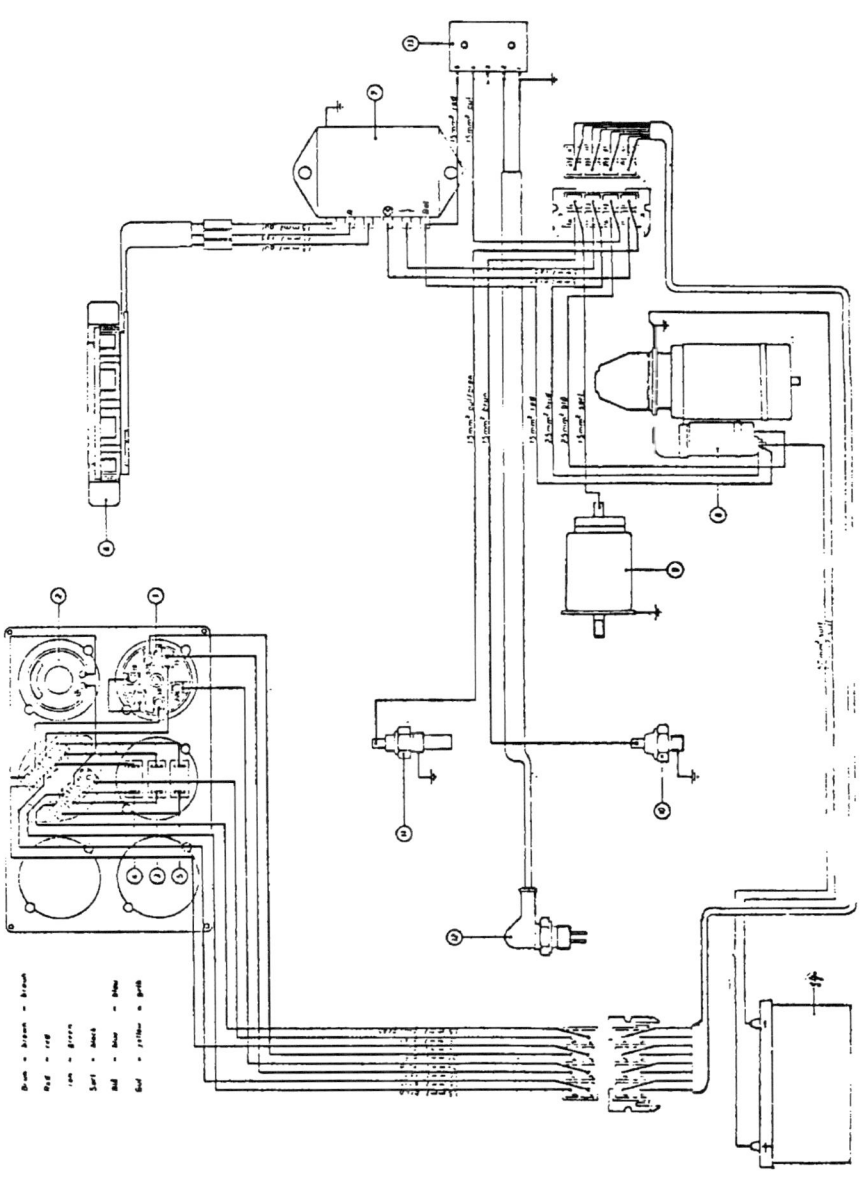

Section R

ZF-gear

BW 3

SECTION S

Sail Drive

Contents

Technical data	page S 3
Zinc anode	page S 3
Outside maintenance	page S 3
Alarm function of double membrane	page S 4
Sectional drawing of S-drive	page S 5
Function of S-drive	page S 6
General - Repairs	page S 7
Dismantling of S-drive	page S 7
Reassembly of S-drive	page S 9
Checking of clearance of tooth flanke	page S 12
Checking of tooth contact patterns of gear wheels	page S 12
Reassembling of S-drive (final assembling)	page S 14
Adjustment of change-over mechanism	page S 16
Fitting of membrane	page S 17
Fitting of propellers	page S 18

Technical Data

Gear reduction "AHEAD"	1.75:1
Gear reduction "ASTERN":	1.75:1
Quality of lub. oil	Hypoid gear oil or Outboard gear oil.
Quantity of lub. oil	0.4 ltr.
Change of lub. oil	once a season.

Zinc Anode

A replaceable zinc anode is fitted at the propeller. Check this anode once or twice a year and replace it as required, all depending on the waters you are sailing in and on the construction of the individual boat.

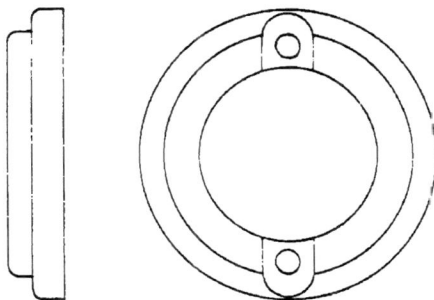

Outside Maintenance

Do not grind thoroughly when careening the boat. Damage to the surface treatment should be treated as soon as possible with special BUKH paint.

The bottom of the boat is often painted with anti-fouling paint and this must not contain copper. Hempels Hard Racing is suitable for this purpose.

The painting of the S-drive is carried out in two stages:

1. Clean the S-drive and paint it with <u>Hempadur HI - Build 4520</u>, which is a green two-component epoxy-polyamid paint. The surface is dry after 4 hours and the paint completely dry after 16 hours and hardened after one week.

S 4

2. Paint the S-drive after the treatment under point 1 with <u>Hempels Poly Emaille 5510</u>, which is a red two-component polyuretanbased enamel with the same times for drying of the paint as mentioned under point 1.

Alarm Function of Double Membrane

A sensing element is fitted in the double membrane. The element is shown on the diagram below. The sensing element is connected with the operating panel and if water penetrates into the double membrane it will release an acoustic alarm.

If you should like to have a lamp fitted as a parallel alarm to the acoustic alarm this may be fitted as indicated with the dot-and-dash line on the sketch.

As a precaution the alarm function should be checked once a year by short-circuiting the connections 1 and 2 on the plastic box placed on the engine next to the multiple plug.

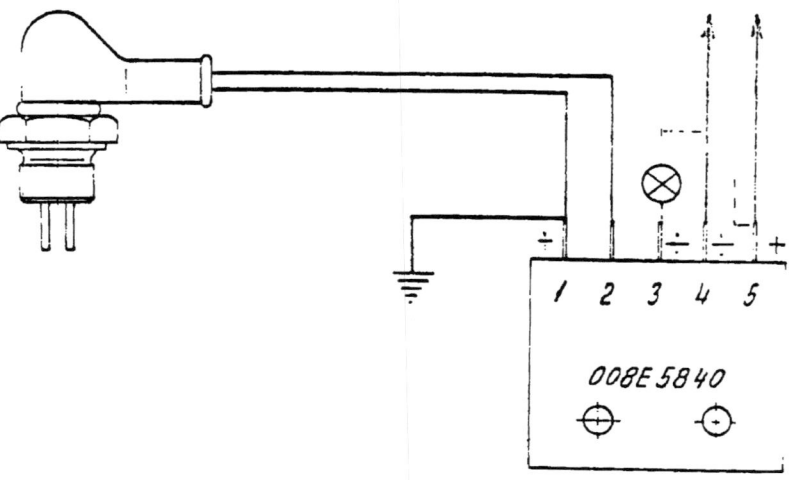

Sectional Drawing of S-drive

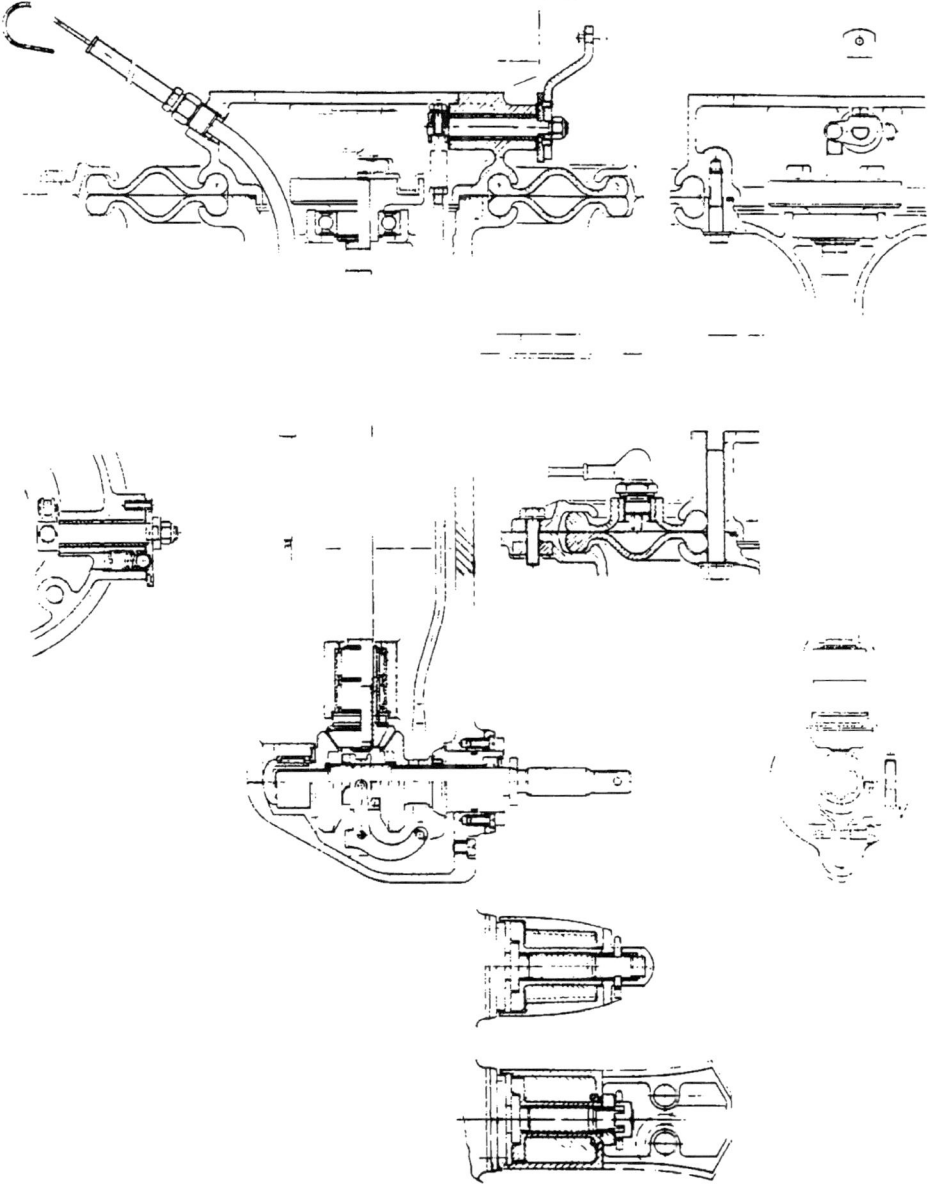

Function of S-drive

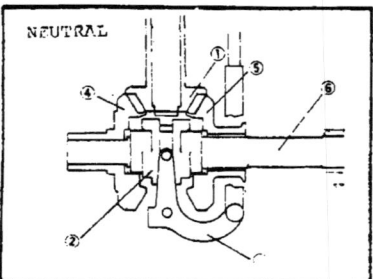
NEUTRAL

1. Driving wheel
2. Shifting claw
3. Shifter yoke
4. Wheel - AHEAD
5. Wheel - ASTERN
6. Propeller shaft

When activating the gear shifting lever from Neutral to Ahead or Astern the shifting claw should be pushed into engagement with the wheel AHEAD or the wheel ASTERN via the shifter yoke.

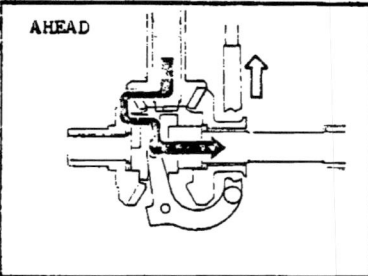
AHEAD

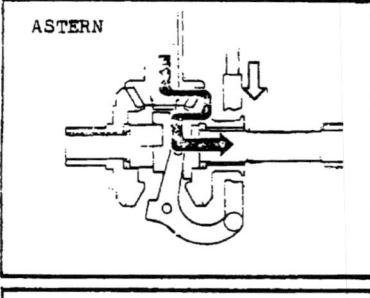
ASTERN

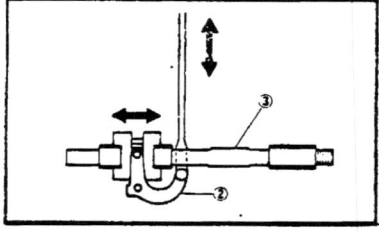

General – Repairs

In order to prevent wrong measurings when adjusting, the parts should normally not be oiled, when being assembled.

Max. permissible temperature when fitting bearings is 140°C.

Difference of temperature when pressing in bearings 80°C.

Dismantling of S-drive after Removal from Engine

The sketches and the text below indicate an overall dismantling of the S-drive, and depending on the components which are to be exchanged, some of the operations can be left out, as a total dismantling of the components is possible, and often more expedient.

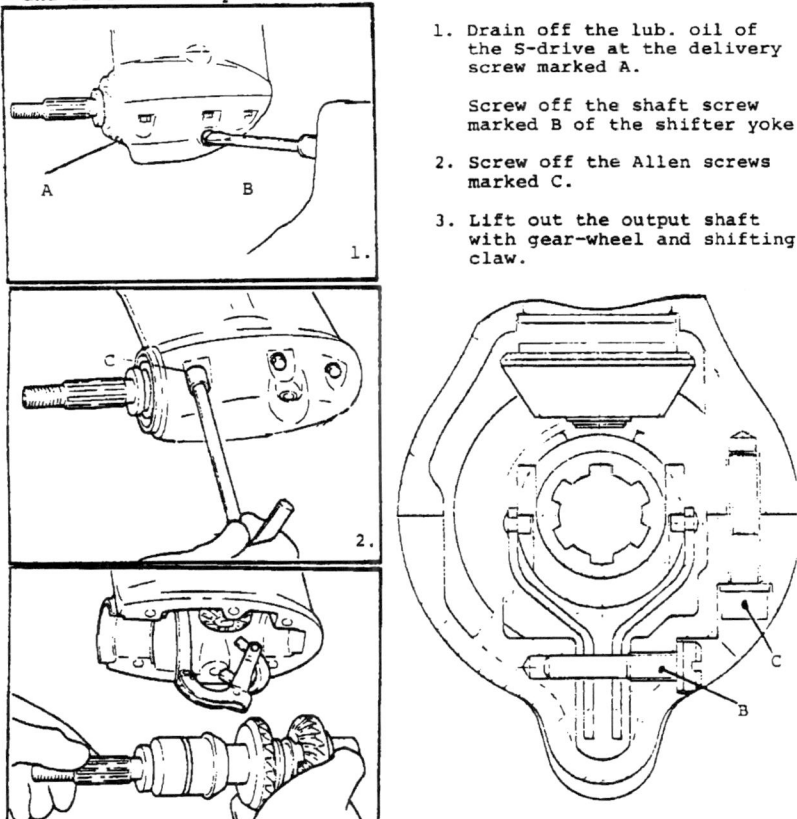

1. Drain off the lub. oil of the S-drive at the delivery screw marked A.

   Screw off the shaft screw marked B of the shifter yoke

2. Screw off the Allen screws marked C.

3. Lift out the output shaft with gear-wheel and shifting claw.

S 8

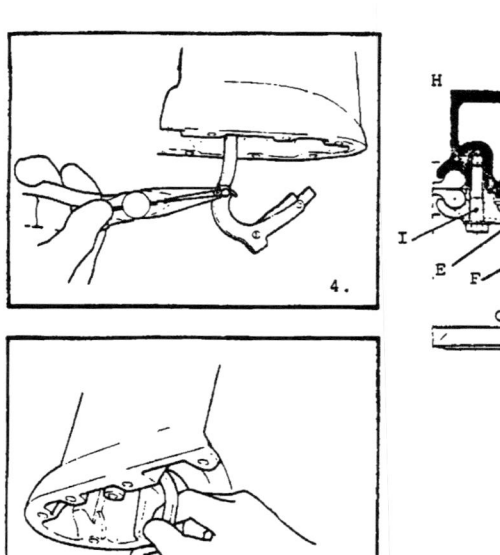

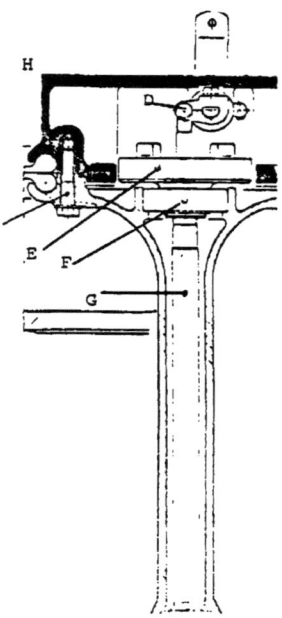

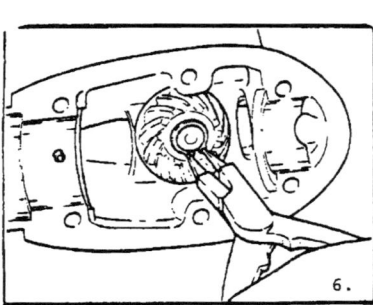

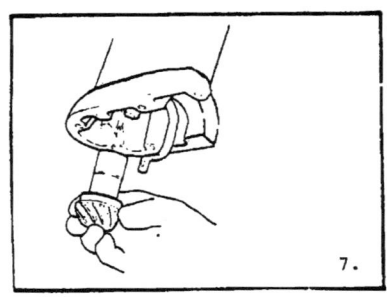

4. Remove the lock pin and take out the shifter yoke.

5. It will often be more expedient to take out the lock pin marked D instead, and then take out the whole gear shifting lever with shifter yoke at a time.

   When the split pin D and the two bolts I have been removed, the intermediate housing H can be lifted out.

   The coupling half marked E with fitted ball bearing can also be lifted up by means of e.g. two screwdrivers and free of the driving shaft marked G.

6. Take out the locking ring of the driving wheel.

7. The driving wheel can then be lifted free of the driving shaft.

   Instead of dismantling as described in points 6 and 7 the driving shaft and driving wheel may be taken out assembled.

S 9

Reassembly of S-Drive

1. Fit one washer pos. 21 (t=1.0 mm) on the driving wheel pos. 19.

2. Fit two washers pos. 27 (t=1.50 mm) between the axial thrust washer of the gear-wheel pos. 24 and the needle bearing pos. 23.

THE COPPER COATING OF THE THRUST BEARING IS TO FACE THE GEAR-WHEEL

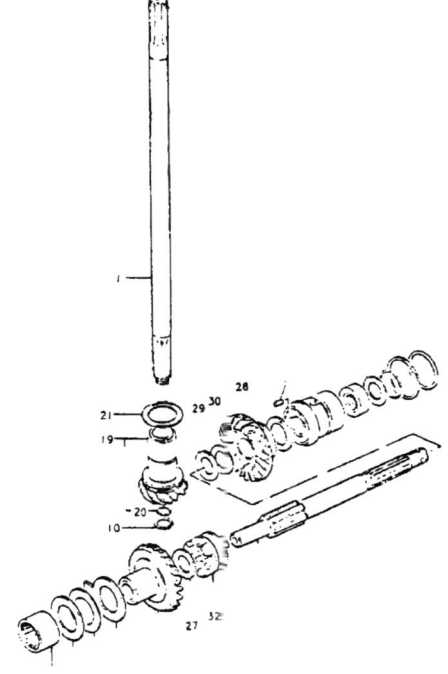

NB: No oil when assembling the S-drive in order to avoid wrong measurings.

S 10

Clearance of flank WHEEL - AHEAD-ASTERN: 0.25-0.50 mm
Axial clearance WHEEL - AHEAD-ASTERN: 0.05 mm (max.)
Axial clearance PROPELLER SHAFT: 0.05-0.15 mm
Torque of screws in bottom part 0.8-1.0 kpm

The position numbers refer to
the drawing on page S 9

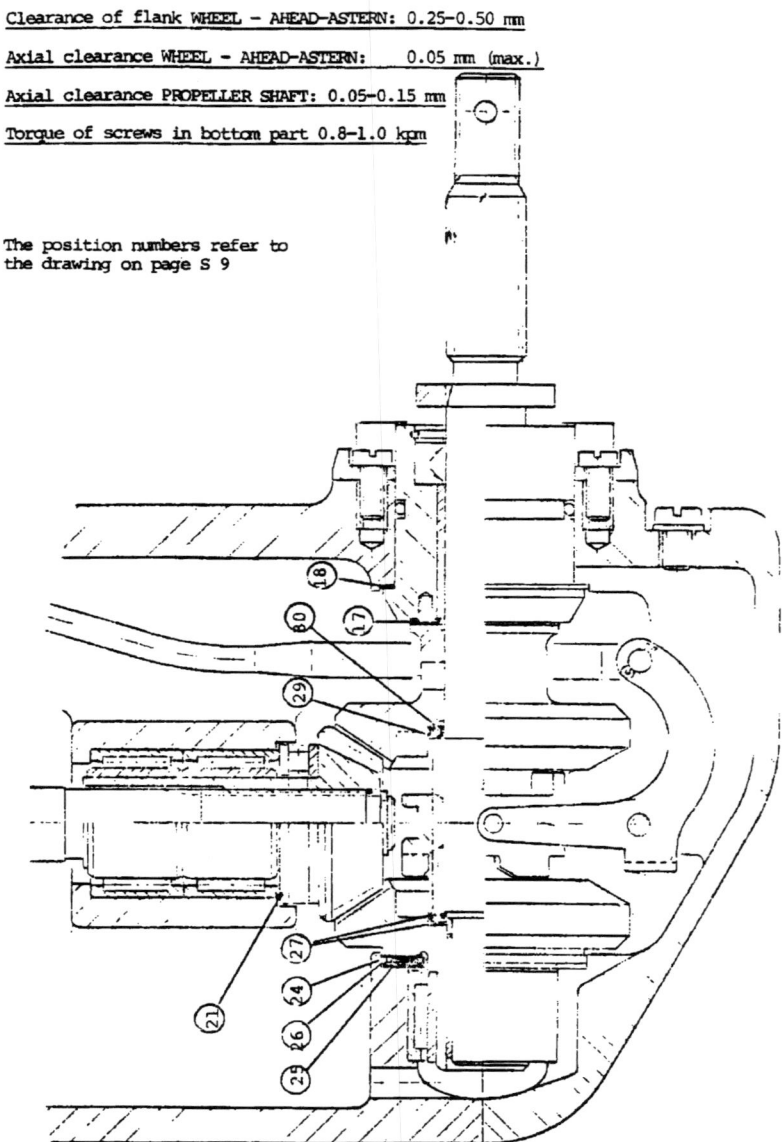

S 11

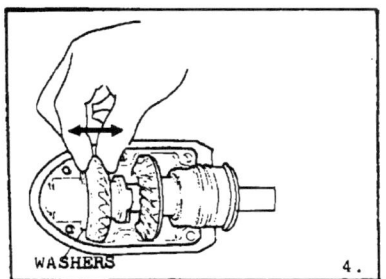

4. Check the axial clearance between the gear-wheel pos. 19 (page S 9) and the gear-wheel pos. 22.

Adjust the clearance to max. 0.05 mm by means of washers.

<u>Washers for adjustment of the clearance are stated in table No. 1 below.</u>

TABLE 1 (WHEEL - AHEAD)

Pos. No.	Thickness	BUKH NO.
25	2.0	620A2164
26	1.5	620A2163
26	1.0	620A2165
26	0.5	620A2161
26	0.1	620A2162

TABLE 2 (WHEEL - ASTERN)

Pos. No.	Thickness	BUKH NO.
18	0.1	620A2167
18	1.5	620A2168
18	2.0	620A2169

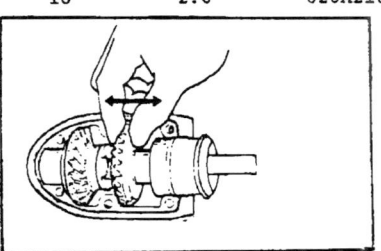

5. Fit the gear-wheel astern pos. 28 on the prop. shaft and carry out a similar adjustment as the one described under point 4.

<u>Washers for adjustment of the clearance are stated in the above table No. 2.</u>

6. When the gear-wheels have been adjusted: Check the <u>axial play of the propeller shaft</u> which should be <u>0.05-0.15 mm</u>.

Washers for adjustment of the axial play of the prop. shaft are stated in table 3 below.

TABLE 3 (PROPELLER SHAFT)

Pos. No.	Thickness	BUKH NO.
29	1.5	620A2152
29	1.0	620A2154
29	0.7	620A2155
30	0.5	620A2153
30	0.1	620A2151

S 12

Check of Clearance of Tooth Flank

1. Fit a dial meter on the gear-wheel of the propeller shaft so that the measuring key fulfils the following requirements:

    A: Point of contact to be approx. in the middle of the tooth flank in the pitch circle.

    B: The key to stand vertically in both the longitudinal as well as in the height direction of the tooth flank.

2. With the small gear-wheel secured, measure the clearance of the tooth flank by turning from stop to stop. The dial meter will then indicate the corresponding clearance of tooth flank.

3. The clearance of the tooth flank which is to be 0.25-0.50 mm is to be adjusted on the front gear-wheel pos. 22 (page S 9) by means of washers as indicated in table 1 (page S 11).

4. Check of the clearance of the tooth flank of the ASTERN wheel is carried out in the same way as by the AHEAD wheel. Washers for adjusting of the ASTERN wheel are indicated in table 2 (page S 11).

Check of Tooth Contact Patterns of Gear Wheel

In order to check whether the gear-wheels "meet perfectly" it is necessary to take an impression of the tooth contact patterns of the wheels.

1. Fit the shaft and the gear-wheel in the propeller housing together with the initially chosen washers.

2. Apply a thin coat of marking paste on 5-6 teeth of the AHEAD wheel.

3. Fit shifting lever, shifter yoke, and shifting fork in the propeller housing (the long part of the leg).

4. Fix the bottom part of the leg to the propeller housing by means of the 6 Allen screws with a torque of 0.8-1.0 kpm.

5. Fit the shaft screw of the shifter yoke (see page S 7 point 1).

6. With the coupling in "AHEAD" position rotate the driving shaft 10 turns clockwise while braking the propeller shaft by hand.

7. Then the tooth contact patterns should be examined visually. See the valuations on page S 13.

S 13

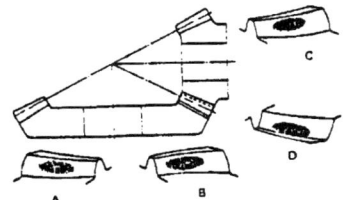

Correct tooth contact pattern indicating that the adjustment of the gear-wheels is correct.

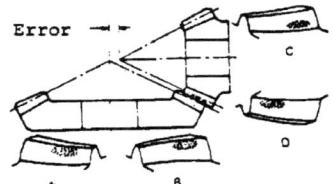

Adjusting error. The picture indicates that some more washers pos. 21 page S 9 are to be fitted (thickness of washers 0.10 mm - see table).

When fitting washers: move the gear-wheel further towards the center line of the big gear-wheel.

After this it may be necessary to move the big gear-wheel in order to obtain correct clearance of tooth flank.

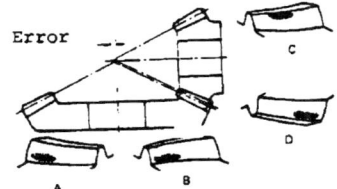

Adjusting error. The picture indicates that some washers have to be removed at pos. 21 page S 9.

Correction of clearance of tooth flank may also be necessary here.

S 14

Reassembling of S-drive

After the adjustment of the gear-wheels the final assembling of the S-drive can be carried out after the following instructions:

1. Fit the thrust washer pos. 17 (page S 9) with the copper-coated side towards the gear-wheel and with the small hole opposite the lock pin in the bearing housing as indicated on the sketch below.

2. Fit the bearing housing so that it is guided by the pin in the propeller housing.

3. Fit the front thrust washer pos. 24 (page S 9) with the copper-coated side towards the gear-wheel and the lock flap against the corresponding "pocket" in the bearing cap as shown on the bottom sketch.

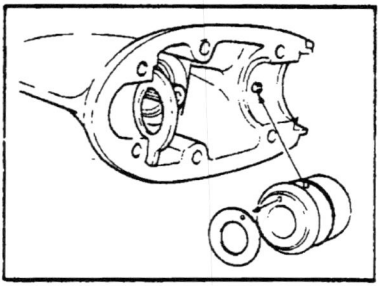

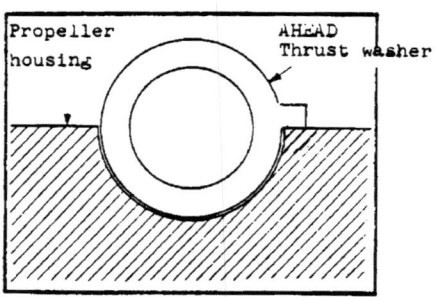

4. Before the bearing housing is fitted in the propeller housing, the surface in an area of about 5 mm on either side of the o-ring should be smeared with sealing compound of a non-hardening type, e.g. CURIL K2 or something similar.
5. Fit shifting lever, fork and yoke in the propeller housing.

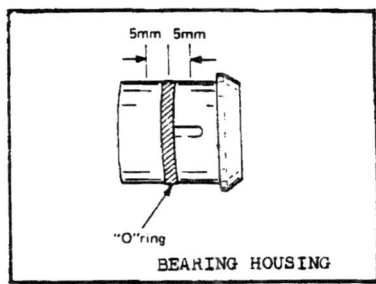
BEARING HOUSING

6. Apply sealing compound to the face of joint of the bearing cap of the same type as indicated under point 4.
7. Fit the bearing cap on the propeller housing with six Allen screws which are to be tightened with 0.8 - 1.0 kpm.

    Smear the screws with LOCK-TITE before fitting them or with a similar locking fluid.
8. Fit gasket and shaft screw in the bearing cap.

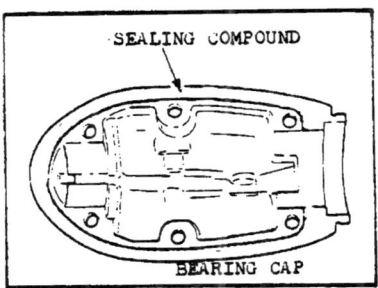
BEARING CAP

S 16

Adjustment of Change-over Mechanism

1. Fit the O-ring marked A on the intermediate housing marked B which is to be fitted to the drive together with the membrane marked C (see page S 17).

2. After this the reversing part can be fitted in the intermediate housing.

3. In order to obtain the same movement on the reversing lever to both AHEAD and ASTERN, the reversing lever should be moved backwards and forwards, while the propeller shaft is turned around.

   Adjust the length of the reversing lever by turning the connecting piece pos. 17 further up or down.

   When the adjustment has been completed the nut pos.18 should be tightened and secure key bolt pos. 14 with the split pin pos. 16.

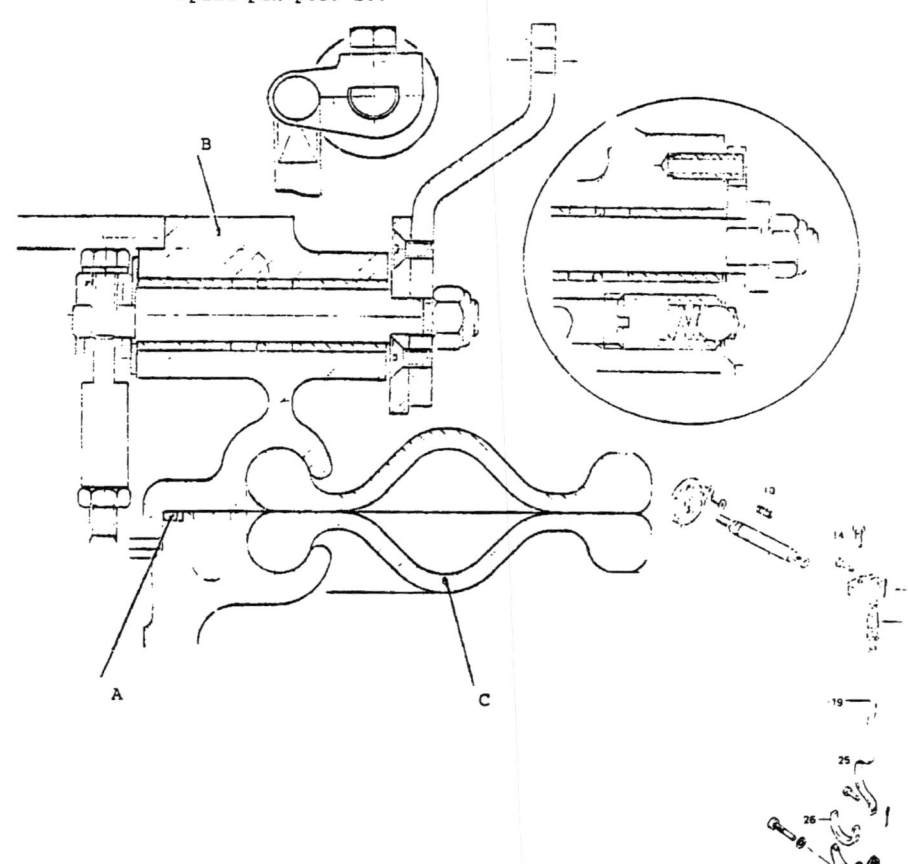

65

Fitting of Membrane

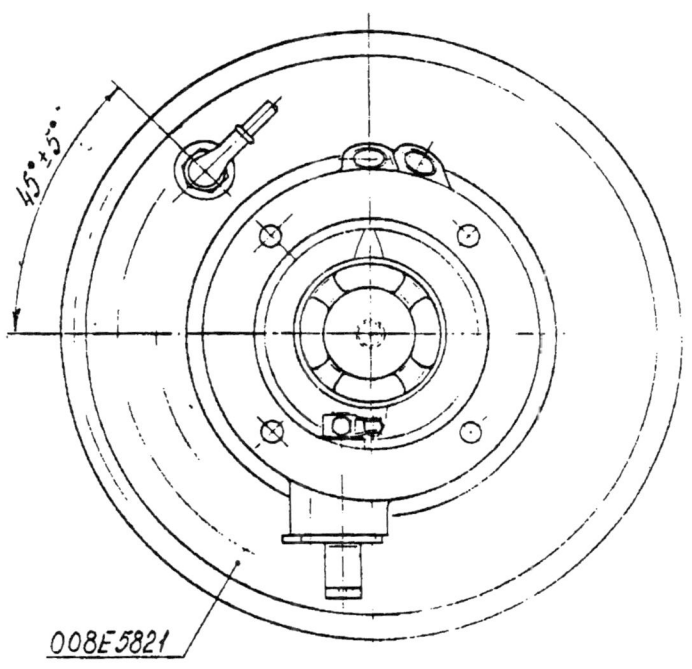

S 18

Fitting of Propellers

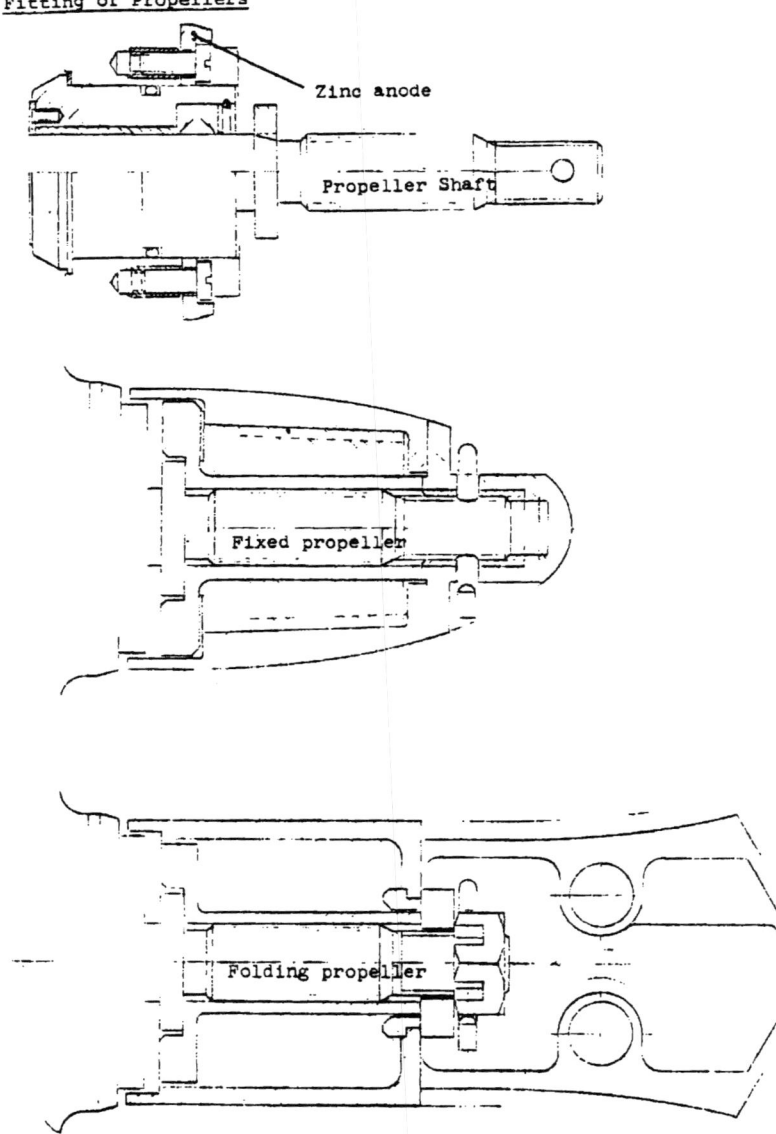

67